I0407181

Submissive

Sissy

Short

Stories

Volume 1

Table of Contents:

Are you almost ready Sissy?

"Are you almost ready honey?" "I don't want to be late tonight, so get your sissy ass in gear." I came out of the bathroom and looked at my wife Cynthia, she was a beautiful woman, a strong woman, a woman who knew what she wanted. I was amazed when she chose me all those years ago in college; she told me that I could be the man she wanted me to be. I had no idea back then what that eventually would mean. Over the years she slowly made me into what she said she wanted and that was a sissy husband. She got off on seeing me in feminine attire, and she really got off on embarrassing me in front of her friends. I myself didn't have any friends, I was totally Cynthia's and she made sure I knew it. She often would have her friends over and would keep me in some slutty maid's outfit and all her friends would laugh at me. They would always lift my skirt to see what Cynthia called my little sissy clit. Tonight was different tonight we were going to visit one of her male friends and I was very nervous about this. As I approached her she turned and asked me. "Did you put it on?" "Is it on good and snug?" Before I could answer she took it upon herself to check and when she didn't find it snug enough to her standings she just slapped me across the face and adjusted it herself. Now put your shoes on and lets go, I don't want to keep him waiting.

As we arrived at the house it took a little effort to keep up with her she was much more used to walking in high heels then I was, the shoes she had picked out for me were now firmly locked onto my feet so I could not take them off. John answered the door just as we started to knock and let us inside his home. My wife gave him a big hug and kissed him quite openly on the mouth, I stood and watched as their tongues entwined. Finally she broke off her long kiss and they proceeded to walk into the living room and sit down on the couch. She then turned to me and introduced me as her husband. John told me how lucky I was and that I had an amazing woman for a wife. I whole heartedly agreed with him and thanked him as I was told I must do. John eyed my shoes a little suspiciously and my wife proceeded to explain to him. "I told you that I would show you that my husband is ok with what I want to do with you, and to further demonstrate this." She turned to me and told me to take off my clothes. At first I was a little hesitant but realized there was no going back now. As I removed my outer clothing I was left standing there in the high heels, stockings with a garter belt, panties and a bra. John looked me up and down and then commented to my wife about how thorough she was, noticing that I didn't have any body hair and that my finger and toe nails were painted bright red to match the lipstick she now always made me wear. "But that's not all" my wife said and reached over and pulled the front of my panties down to show John the chastity belt that my cock was caged in. John looked up at me and told me how impressed he was that I would do all this to make my wife happy. John then turned to her and asked what else she was teaching me. I stood and watched my wife's hand start rubbing John's crotch right there in front of me. It didn't take long before John's zipper was down and his pants were off. She then turned to me and told me to make John's cock hard for her. I was soon down on my knees face to face with another man's cock and my wife guided it into my mouth. She then began to kiss John passionately as I sucked this man's cock. I could feel it growing bigger and thicker inside of my warm mouth. It was much bigger then my own cock which no matter how hard it tried could not get an erection in the chastity belt. When my wife was satisfied she told me to stop and to go clean John's bathroom. As I walked away I saw her slide one leg over his lap and impale herself upon John's large cock. I entered John's bathroom and could hear the sounds of my wife getting fucked by John. She had already came once by the time I found what I needed to clean John's toilet. I worked in the bathroom for about an hour when I heard my wife calling me to rejoin them. They were sitting on the couch again my wife still had her legs up in the air. As I came close to her she just simply looked up at me and told me that John had cum quite a bit inside her pussy and that I needed to get down there and lick his cum up. John scooted close to her and watched as I knelt between her legs and began to lick the gobs of his cum up from the outside of my wife's pussy, I then placed my tongue at her entrance and saw her push out a few more big globs that she smiled at me as I swallowed them down. John was tickled pink by all this he thought it was so funny watching a husband swallow his wife's lovers load. I continued to lick her as they spoke to each other. I heard John ask her how long she was going to keep me in chastity. She responded by stating well you told me that you would not fuck me unless my husband's dick was out of the picture so I guess as long as you keep giving me your big stiff one, his little dick will stay locked up. Don't you want your husband to have release. Of course I do John, but he will have to learn to cum from me penetrating his ass. John looked a little confused and she reached into her bag and pulled out a big strap on. She told me to stop licking her pussy and to clean John's cock up. She got up and came around behind me as I took John's wilted but still bigger then mine cock into my mouth. I felt my panties pulled down and without hesitation my wife slid the big cock into my ass, I screamed into John's cock and the vibration made it start to swell again. My wife started with slow strokes but was soon fucking me harder then I had ever been fucked before. Meanwhile John's cock was fully erect again and when my wife grabbed me by the hips and really gave me some deep penetration I felt my little caged cock start dripping cum onto John's floor and then I felt my mouth fill with another load of John's cum.

Ball Beating

We were lying in bed, she was cuddled up next to me, it was very nice. Her name was Julia and she was hot as hot could be. I heard her whisper in my ear to close my eyes and that I would get a big surprise. Naturally I did just that and she raised my hands above my head as we laid on the bed and I heard the hand cuffs click on my wrists. We had played this game before, and it was a good game or at least I thought it would be, but I was very wrong. She started to play with my nipples, toying with them pulling on them gently, with my eyes still closed I couldn't see her click the little clamps in place that were attached to a small pulley on the wall. She slowly pulled that rope until I started to whimper as my nipples were pulled straight up, I arched my back to reduce the pressure on them and she tied off the rope, my eyes were open now with a look of shock on them. Julia just waved a finger at me saying that I was a bad boy for opening my eyes and I needed to be punished for that. She laid next to my side continuing to play with the strings that were attached to my nipple each time she plucked the string it sent shivers down my spine. She giggled at my predicament, as I felt her left leg sliding up and down mine. That felt exquisite since she was wearing black silk stockings, each time her leg raised a little further up my own. Then I heard her whisper if I was ready for my punishment, and before my head had completed its nod, I felt her bring her leg up sharply as her knee slammed hard against my balls. I never saw it coming and the pain was excruciating, she laughed out loud as I couldn't get away with my hands and nipples tied up tightly. I felt her hand gently rubbing my balls holding them in her hand, slowly the pain started to subside, but that was short lived. As once again her knee met my groin, this time I felt the tears start to well up in my eyes. I begged her to stop but she just laughed again this time she raised herself up and proceeded to move my cock up to my belly. She produced some duct tape and taped it pointing at my belly button. She then turned her full attention to my balls, she listed out a number of things that I had done in the past week that had upset her and that she was going to get some retribution for her troubles. She then proceeded to give my balls ten good swats with her right open hand. The tears were no longer in my eyes but now running down my cheeks as I begged her to stop. I felt her left hand wrap around my balls, encircling them and pulling them tightly away from my body, that didn't hurt to much and I found a certain amount of pleasure in with that. Then I watched as she made a fist with her right hand and proceeded to punch my balls ten more times, she told me later it was ten because by the time she got to six I had passed out. She told me the next day that if I didn't improve she would have her doctor friend come over and instead of hurting my balls she would have them removed from my ball sack and she would put them in a jar on the shelf in the front room for everyone to see.

Debbie was the best girlfriend I had ever had

Debbie was the best girlfriend I had ever had, she meant the world to me, and I too her. Or at least I thought I did. She had begun bossing me around, I didn't mind that too much because most of the things she was bossing me around about were truly something I needed a little push with to get done. I mean after so many times of coming over to her house to do her laundry you would think that I would know how she likes her laundry done by now. Each time I made a mistake she would just give me more and more complicated things to do. Now I not only have to do her laundry but I have to iron each article of clothing and fold it and put it away, it takes me hours to do this. She told me how much she appreciated the work that I do for her, and she does reward me when I am done. Usually she will be naked in the bedroom and when I have completed my task and closed the last drawer as I put away the final piece of clothing she will have me strip down and kneel next to her on the bed. "You have been such a good boyfriend, I am so proud of the way you take care of my things." She will say. Then she will take my cock and begin to stroke it up and down, she will get real close to it and I can feel her hot breath on the head of my cock. "I don't know what I would do without you, I am so lucky to have such a pretty boyfriend, who knows how to treat his lady." She would say. By then my cock is hard and I am so horny since the last time, it usually doesn't take me very long before I start spurting cum all over her tits. She then laughs with delight as smiles up at me with my spurting cock in her hand. "Oh that was a good one honey, you did so well, and you almost lasted five minutes. Go get a nice

hot wet towel and you can clean me off."
She would say.

Things stayed like that for quite a while, I was never allowed to penetrate Debbie and she never seemed to want to be. There were times I would be doing her laundry and she would be on the bed with her large dildo slowly sliding it in and out of her pussy, she wouldn't pay any attention to my comings and goings while she was fucking herself with the dildo, her head was usually tilted back and the moaning and groaning was very loud, I am sure the neighbors heard it. She had told me once that she screamed loudly just for me, so that the neighbors would know what a real man I was and how good I was in bed.

When Debbie had said that I couldn't help but ask her when I was going to get to make her cum like that with my cock inside her instead of the dildo? She laughed for a bit, "Oh honey your cock is not big enough to make me feel the way the dildo does, and besides you would cum to quickly and then what would I have, a pussy filled with cum and no orgasm for me. You wouldn't want that now would you?" I know it was a silly question for her to ask but yet I still found myself bowing my head in submission to her and telling her that, no I would not want that. "Now be a good pretty boyfriend and clean the kitchen and when you come back I will give you a big surprise." As you can imagine I was off to go clean the kitchen, because I wanted my new surprise.

The kitchen wasn't that dirty and I quickly cleaned it up, when I got back to her room she was ready for me. "Well your surprise is twofold the first you will receive a spanking from me because of your question earlier, and the second I think it is time to move you to the next level and fill you in on a few things" She smiled. I stripped down and I crawled across the bed and across her lap. I could feel the heat coming up from between her legs as my cock laid between her legs, it was immediately getting hard as it brushed against her pubic hair. I had thought she was going to spank me with her hand, I never saw the wooden hairbrush until I felt it strike across my butt cheeks, it hurt like a mother fucker, by the tenth slap of the brush the tears were flowing down my face and I felt so ashamed for questioning her before, ten more strokes of the brush and I was squirming and balling. When she finally stopped spanking me I looked at her and she had a big smile on her face. "You have to understand that I am the boss, and I make the rules and the decisions, you may be my boyfriend but you are beneath me and will do what I say. Do you understand?" She asked. Yes Debbie I understand you make the rules and I will do what you say. "Good I am so glad I don't have to spank you again, because I would have, I would have done it as many times as was necessary to make you understand." She told me. "Now I guess I should speak plainly to you and we can go on from there. I know I call you my boyfriend and I know how much you like the idea that I am your girlfriend but we need to be honest with ourselves you are not really my boyfriend and I am certainly not your girlfriend, if we were, you would be fucking me instead of being spanked and doing my laundry don't you think?" She asked. I didn't know what to say as I was still sobbing from the spanking so I just nodded my head. "Good I am so glad that is out in the open I was so afraid you would have a hard time understanding that. So what you really are, is my submissive, which means I am your boss, or to be more bluntly your owner in a sense. Now I have not really gone about this in the proper method, in a sense I have been leading you on over the last few months and all that so I am going to give you the option after we are done talking to leave or serve, it will be up to you. First though you will need to know what will be expected of you if you do decide to serve, first off just like before you will keep my household spotless and do all the chores you normally do now to please me, and if it does not please me I will beat you like before or worse. There will be times I will be bringing real men home who will fuck me, sometimes right in front of you and you will have to be quiet while you stand there and watch me get a big cock in my pussy, you may be asked to clean up after the man cums inside of me, or maybe I will have you suck his cock to get him hard for me, there are many different things that could happen but I wanted you to know the basics that I will be getting fucked and you will not be fucking me. I might even dress you up as a little slut for my own amusement.

So do you still want to be my boyfriend? I was once again at a loss for words and simply nodded my head.

The doorbell rang. She smiled and then handed me a toothbrush and told me to go clean her bathroom.

I started cleaning the bathroom on my hands and knees when I heard her re-enter the bedroom this time with her guest. It wasn't long before I heard her moaning and groaning and new that this was one of her friends who was getting to fuck her. I continued to clean the bathroom with the toothbrush; it was about a half an hour later when I heard her call me back. As I entered back into the bedroom she was laying on the bed and a man was there next to her, they were both naked so I averted my eyes. "You can look, in fact I want you to look, I want you to cum up here on the bed and so my friend John here can see how you are a good little slut, he wants to watch another man lick his cum from my pussy.

As I crawled between her legs being so close to her pussy for the first time, I was amazed at how beautiful it looked, even though it was covered and oozing cum from its lips. "Go ahead and give my pussy a big kiss." She told me. As I placed my lips upon her lips she flexed her diaphragm muscle and I got a mouthful of John's cum. It was still warm from being inside of her, it didn't taste bad but it was weird to have to do this, it was so against me being a man, but I continued to lick her clean swallowing it all. Then she had me take John's cock in my mouth and clean that off, the time it took me to clean her out and the sucking of his cock just got him hard again and he pushed me off and fucked Debbie again creating a new mess for me to clean up. Later after John had left Debbie took my cock in her hand and told me what a good job I had done while she slowly stroked it and again it didn't take me long before I spurted my cum again all over her tits, though this time there would be no hot wet towel as she leaned back on the bed and I leaned forward to lick my own cum off of her tits.

First you wear pink

I couldn't believe I was doing this but a bet was a bet, and I lost so here I was sliding on a pair of pink silky panties, my wife was enjoying the sight of me sliding them over my rapidly hardening cock. "See I knew you would like wearing them, look how hard your cock is." She said as she lowered her own fingers in between her legs. I started to protest about the pink stockings, asking if I could at least wear black ones. "Absolutely not, all girls start out with pink everything, and since this is your first set they have to be pink." She said while giggling under her breath. I would not admit it to her but I felt very sexy when I stood up and could feel the stockings against my legs. "Here is the last piece for your new underwear ensemble." She said as she handed me the pink bra. She had to help me with the straps and the fastening of it, as she reached around and played with my nipples through the silky fabric, I could feel my cock straining against the pink panties as she pinched and pulled my nipples.

It was off to work then as she patted my ass telling me to have a good day at work and that I better hope no one sees what I have on or who knows what might happen. I had that on my mind on the ride into work, what if someone saw and confronted me about it. I would have to be careful. It felt very strange as I entered the men's room, I didn't want to use the urinal because I was afraid someone might see my pink panties, not that men do much talking or looking in the bathroom, it is usually do your business and get out, very different I imagine from what goes on in the ladies room. I decided to use a stall instead, as I unbuckled my pants and let them fall to the floor, I was keenly aware of my undergarments, there I was all in pink as I sat down I realized that if someone looked under the stall they would see pink stockings so I pulled my pants back up to my knees as I sat there. I couldn't help myself thinking about how my nipples had felt when she had played with them and I found my hands coming to my breasts and rubbing the nipples through the silky fabric again, they were rock hard and it felt really good as I ran my fingers roughly over them. It was obvious that my cock liked it as well as it grew rapidly, I thought about playing with myself, but decided against it, it was too early in the morning and I had work to do.

My secretary greeted me at my office with a cup of coffee for me, thanking her I asked her what was on the agenda for today, she told me I had two meetings but most of the day was free. We had had a fling or two on a couple of business trips but we realized from the beginning that it was just some fun and neither of us had expectations of anything other than a good roll in the hay every once and awhile. "There is something different about you today, not sure what it is but I will figure it out" She smiled as she left my office. That thought made me feel a little bit nervous but I was sure I could keep it a secret for the day, it was only one day, so I was sure there wouldn't be any problems.

As the day wore on I couldn't stop thinking about how naughty it felt to be outwardly dressed as a fully functioning masculine male, and underneath knowing that I was wearing such frilly feminine attire. My cock was hard for most of the morning and I was very aware of its presence in my pink panties. My wife called right before lunch and asked me how my day was going, I told her that everything was ok so far, I let her know that I was enjoying the feeling and explained how I was very horny and felt rather naughty about wearing the panties, stockings, and bra, but I was having fun with it.

It was right after lunch when my secretary came back in with a big smile on her face as she closed and locked my office door. She came right around and sat on my desk. "So I have been thinking about what is different about you today, and I think I figured it out." I simply smiled at her feeling safe with my secret. "I was listening on the phone when you were talking to your wife and I know all about how you are wearing ladies under garments under your business suit." She said with an evil grin. I never felt so frightened in my life, I felt like my whole world was going to come to an end. "You must have been mistaken there is no way I would wear ladies clothes" I tried to lie my way out of it. She reached out quickly beneath my jacket and felt my chest and easily felt the bra under my shirt. "Now you shouldn't have lied to me about that, you should have just come clean, we have a very good relationship you and I and it doesn't bother me a bit, in fact I think it is kind of sexy." She said with a frown on her face. "I want to see them take off your clothes." She told me. I simply refused; I was not going to be humiliated in front of her, in front of anybody for that matter. "You will take your clothes off and let me see you in your ladies underwear or I will go straight to Human Resources and tell them all about our little encounters on our business trips." I felt trapped like a cat in a corner, and I couldn't fight my way out of this one.

As the last piece of my clothing was

removed she made me stand in front of her, while she sat on the office couch. "You look so pretty in pink, your wife chose well. It is making me very horny just looking at you dressed like that." She then proceeded to pull her skirt up and began playing with herself, she began rubbing her clit and then slid a finger inside of her pussy. My cock which had been semi hard all day was now fully hard and the head of my cock was peeking through the top of my panties. She reached up and pulled my panties down and took the head of my cock in her mouth, looking at her red lips as they slid down my cock was amazing. We had never done anything in the office before and I was still very nervous standing in front of her in only pink panties, stockings and a bra, but I was getting my cock sucked on. She was exceptionally good at it as well as she took me deeper and deeper into her mouth. It didn't take long before she was moaning and she stopped sucking my cock as she came from her finger manipulation of her clit. She pulled down her skirt and proceeded to stand up. "Hey what about me, are you not going to finish what you started?' I asked her. "Your wife is going to expect a good fucking when you get home and you don't want to blow your load here at the office and have to explain that you have no self-control now do you?" I knew she was right but I still had a raging hard on. She got really close to me and as she looked me in the face her one hand slowly went down my chest until it was level with my crotch. I never saw it coming but she rapidly slapped my balls through the panties like five or six times, I almost collapsed from the pain. "You don't even know what you are now do you, you don't know what it is called, do you?" She looked down on me as I was crouched from the pain emanating from my balls. "What do you mean?" Your wife wants to turn you into a sissy husband, and I think it is a great idea so this is what you are going to do when you get home, when the subject comes up you are going to tell you wife that you enjoyed the experience of today and that you want to keep doing it, that you like the idea of being more feminine and that she should find other ways and things to do to control you and remove more of your masculinity. If you don't do this HR will find out all about how you treat your secretary.

The rest of the day I was even more nervous about the day's activities, when the day ended I made my way back to my car for the drive home. Of course my secretary was leaning against my car and simply reminded me that I had better be dressed appropriately tomorrow as well.

I found my wife in the bedroom when I got back; she had been waiting for me just as my secretary had said she would. She was already playing with her dildo sliding it in and out of her pussy as I got undressed. She was so excited to see me in my pink under garments with my cock already hard as I slid between her legs the feeling of her stockings rubbing against my own stockings was very intense. Then she began to pinch my nipples as my cock slid inside of her pussy. "You look so pretty honey all in pink, just like a little sissy, I really like that you did this for me today, most guys never get a chance to understand how sexy it is to wear panties and stockings. Did you enjoy yourself today?" I thought about what my secretary had told me I knew that I had no choice but at the same time, I really did enjoy my day today.

"Yes I enjoyed the feeling, I felt very naughty and it was so exciting the feelings I had just at the most simplest movements I was reminded just what a naughty little sissy I was." The next part was the hard part. "Can we keep doing this, I mean can you keep making me do this, can you make me into a sissy husband, I mean the whole works, whatever you want me to do or wear I will, I want to be your little sissy husband." I told her. "You don't know how happy that makes me feel, I was so hoping that you liked the experience, I wasn't sure how I was going to talk you into continuing the experience, I have so many ideas on how to make you even more of a sissy, some things you may still have a problem with but I am sure that once we get you down the road a little bit you won't have the mind blocks to even more naughty experiences." I kept fucking her, and she kept pinching my nipples telling me what a little sissy slut I was for wearing stockings, and how a real man wouldn't have let this happen to him, and how I was going to need to be trained and possibly punished until I learned how to truly satisfy her needs. The nipple pulling and the dirty talk was just too much and I exploded inside of her filling her.

As I rolled over exhausted from the days experiences my wife cuddled up next to me and explained how we would be getting rid of all my male underwear and socks that from now on I would only wear panties and stockings. She then said we will have to figure out something to do with my boi clit, and how she was researching some devices that would do exactly what she wanted and that I was to not worry my little sissy head about it.

I knew my life had taken a change, but I wasn't sure if it was for the better or worse just yet, but I was interested to see what would happen next.

Forced by my wife

I wasn't really sure what had happened, but I found myself laying naked face down on the bed, my wife was lying on top of me with a fistful of my hair.

"You are going to be my little bitch from here on out" she yelled at me.

"I am not going to take any more of your masculine shit, from now on I am going to be the one wearing the pants" she continued.

I was so taken aback I didn't have any response for the words she was saying.

"Just so you know who is boss from this point on I am going to show you who has the cock in the family now" she said with an evil grin.

As that thought was sinking in to my brain I felt her press something against my ass and as it dawned on me that she was going to penetrate me the pain of having my asshole forced open as what must have been a large plastic cock enter into me. I began to scream from the pain, this however did not seem to cause my wife any concern in fact it was quite the opposite.

"Go ahead and scream you little pussy, I am still going to fuck you and this is only the beginning" she laughed at me.

The head of the cock was now inside of me, the pain was extreme as I had never had anything go inside of me except maybe a finger when my wife was giving me a blowjob. I could feel her pushing against me.

"This is making me so hot seeing you beneath me, just watching this cock slide deeper into you, my pussy is so wet seeing you this way" she said.

The pressure she was putting on her end of the plastic cock finally overcame the resistance my asshole was placing against the head of the cock and I felt it move into me a few inches more. The pain once again spread throughout my body and another scream left my lips.

"Keep screaming you little girl, you never realized how much it could hurt having a cock shoved up your ass, you didn't seem to care about that when you suggested having anal sex with me in the past. You never saw the tears in my eyes after you shot your load up my asshole" She angrily said to me.

Now she was pulling it out and pushing it back in with a certain anxious rhythm each time she pushed it deeper into me. She released my hair and I felt both of her hands on my hips she wasn't happy enough with the pushing she wanted me to feel even more like a little slut by pulling my ass onto her cock.

"Look at that the little slut's asshole is relaxing and is now accepting the cock up his ass. Now that I have you in this position, our relationship will never be the same you realize that don't you. From now on when we fuck it will be like this, and you will learn to enjoy being fucked in the ass because that is the only sex you will get from me from now on" She said.

"Why are you doing this honey, I love you. Please don't do this. I begging you to stop please" I pleaded with her.

"It is too late for that now, I am sick of your typical male requests, it is time for you to understand that I am in charge" she responded.

Throughout all of this I could feel her stockings rubbing against my legs that were between hers, and her long finger nails were digging into my sides as I could now tell she was fully inside of me as I could feel her thighs touching my own when she thrust into me. My own cock was rock hard which startled me more than almost anything else.

"Look the little slut likes having his asshole raped by his wife, see how hard your cock is, you can't even get your cock that hard when you fuck me. I guess there is only one way you enjoy your cock getting hard and that is by me pounding your ass."

I felt her hand reach around and grab my hard cock roughly as she continued to thrust deeply into my ass. The thrusting was too much for me to handle and the simple touch of her hand sent my cock over the edge and I started cum all over her hand as she banged my ass even harder knowing that I was cumming.

"Look at how much the little slut enjoyed being fucked in his ass by a girl, look at all that cum on my hand. You better turn around and lick all of your cum up off my hand before I pull this cock out of your ass."

I turned to see her glistening hand before my face and with tears still in my eyes I began to suck the cum off of each finger as she watched with a big smile on her face.

When I completed the task she unceremoniously withdrew the large cock from my ass in one motion causing me to jump. My asshole felt like it was on fire and at the same time I felt somewhat sad that it was over.

I rolled over as my wife came back into the room from cleaning herself up.

"So honey is that what you wanted, did you enjoy a little role reversal, how did I do, was I mean enough towards you? I really enjoyed the feeling it gave me to take you like that."

"It was amazing" I told her. "You really had me scared there for a bit with all that talk in the beginning."

"I wasn't kidding about that part sweetheart, I think we should continue this for a while, I enjoyed it, you enjoyed it, I think it will do our relationship good for us to take turns with who controls the cock, and since we have been married for five years, I think the next five years will have me fucking you like the little slut you are" She smiled.

I thought she was just kidding around, but I soon found out that she was serious about the whole thing. It's been almost a year now, and she fucks me every night, she has gotten a cock that is at least twice the size of that first one, and she even makes me wear women's clothing now around the house. She has some regular friends that come over and fuck her quite regularly, though I haven't had a chance to fuck her since that night. Every once and awhile when they want to fuck her in the ass, I get to stand in for her and regularly have a real man's cock up my ass. In fact one of them comes over to see me on a regular basis; my wife doesn't seem to mind she thinks it will do me good to have a boyfriend since I am going to be a little slut for four more years.

Giving into my wife and her friends

As I hung up the phone with my wife, I could believe how lucky I was. I wasn't sure how the conversation was going to go, she had caught me wearing her stockings and panties last night and she didn't take it very well, I tried to explain to her that I found it very erotic to put them on, she looked at me like I was some sort of a freak. I ended up sleeping on the couch that night; I really thought that this was going to end our relationship. When she called me at the office I was sure she was going to tell me she was leaving me or something like that, but instead she told me that she had talked to one of her friends about it and she realized that it was just me playing out some kinky fantasies. She told me that she understood and wanted to explore this side of me and that she wasn't angry anymore that she was just caught off guard by walking in on me wearing her underwear. I breathed out a sigh of relief at that, and then she hit me with a bombshell. She had a few errands to run and would be home a little late but she wanted me to dress up in as much stuff as I wanted to and that I should tie myself to the bed spread eagle as best I could so that I would be ready for her to play with me when she got home.

My mind was racing all day trying to understand this turn of events, but at the same time my cock was rock hard anticipating my dream of including my wife in my secret fantasies. When I got home and entered the bedroom she had laid out some very sexy stuff, things I wouldn't even touch that belonged to her. I picked up her fishnet stockings and garter belt and after undressing quickly slide the garter belt on and then the stockings they felt so amazing on my legs and after a little difficulty clipped the garter belt to them. I put her black bra on and she even left out those little things girls used to make the boobs look bigger. The little poofy skirt was the finishing touch. I was able to tie my ankles to the bedposts and even able to tie one wrist to the other one as I lay there face down on the bed awaiting her arrival.

I heard the front door open and my wife came into the room and quickly tied my loose hand to the bed and then tightened up all the other knots I made so that I was stretched pretty good across the bed. She slipped the blindfold over my eyes and then I started to hear other voices in the house as well, this made me very nervous, they were girls voices and when they entered the bedroom I could hear them giggling and laughing. "Look at the pathetic bastard, I couldn't believe he actually went through with it, He should have known better then to trust a pissed off wife." As I started to speak up my wife quickly inserted ball gag into my mouth and tied it off. A pillow was slid under my belly as the girls rummaged through some shopping bags. "I think you might as well put this on right now so he understands the position he is in." I felt my wife's hand slid a ring around my cock and balls, it was incredibly tight, something was applied to my cock and then I felt something slipped over it and then I heard a click. "There now that you have that in place there really isn't anything the pathetic little bastard can do if he ever wants to be able to touch his cock again. "Did you hear that little click honey, that was a chastity device, and it was attached with a lock and I have the only key, it will keep you from touching yourself, in fact it will stop you from even getting an erection. Do you like your little game now you little bitch, or should I say you are my little bitch now. I think we need a little demonstration." The other voices came closer and I felt the bra come off and then fingers were rubbing my nipples. The voices were close to my ears, very sexy voices that I didn't recognize. "Such a sexy little sissy boy, wearing your wife's stockings" It went on and on, the pulling and pinching of my nipples my cock was pushing against the cage that it was in, and the pain of my erection being prevented was unbearable. They all got a good laugh out of my torment. "I think its time that this little slut finds out what it feels like to be fucked since he so much wants to experience being a girl" Some lubricant was applied to my asshole and then one by one they took turns raping my ass. I wasn't sure when the tears started rolling down my eyes behind the blindfold. They must have fucked my ass for an hour and a half. When they were done with that, they slid a butt plug into my ass which was stretched out by the workout they gave it. I heard my wife's voice again. "I hoped you enjoyed that, because that is the only type of sex you are going to have for quite a while you little slut." Your cock will be kept locked up for at least six months so don't even ask me about release until Christmas. My girlfriends and I have decided to go out and have a few drinks as we discuss what we should do to you next. We are also going to see if we can find a real man for me to fuck since you will be locked up for a while. They say that I should make you lick me clean after I get fucked by a real man, would you like that honey, is that naughty enough for you. I can't wait to see you lick another man's cum out of my pussy."

Before she left she pushed a button and the butt plug began to vibrate and my cock tried once again to get hard.

"The batteries should run out after a few hours." She said as I heard the door to the bedroom close.

Hot girlfriend who likes me as I am

We had been dating for three weeks, and I hadn't made a move on her, I have to admit I was shy, and she was simply gorgeous. The evening had gone well and we were headed back to her place, at the door I stopped to give her a goodnight kiss, but she was having none of it and pulled me into her home by my tie. Clothes started hitting the floor in the living room and I watched as her dress slipped to the floor, she was amazing to look at, she was all in black lingerie with stockings and a garter belt. My cock was rock hard in my pants. She fell back on the couch and I watched as she removed her panties and exposed her baby smooth crotch. I was on my knees and my tongue was in her snatch in seconds. Her hands were on the back of my head guiding my tongue to the spots that made her feel the most pleasure. Sliding a finger inside of her pussy looking for her g-spot I was quickly rewarded with increased moaning and further pressure upon the back of my head. I continued to lick her lips and encircle her clit with tongue, she was in another world and when she came she came and squirted on my face. I had never experienced that and was a little caught off guard by it, but continued to lick her. The next words out of her mouth was I want your cock inside of me. Sliding my pants off I was on my knees sliding my hard cock into her pussy. She felt the tip of my cock at her opening and wrapped her legs around me pulling me as close to her as possible. I began to thrust in and out of her and she did not respond in the same fashion as when I was licking her to multiple orgasms. I continued to push as deep inside of her as I could go, and she started to look at me in a quizzical manner. Then she stopped me and I withdrew from her and I watched as she reached down in the dark of the room and I felt her hand on my hard cock. Why didn't you tell me your cock was so small, I sat back on my legs as my small cock slipped from her grasp. Your cock is like only three inches long when its hard, I couldn't even feel it inside of me. I can't believe you didn't tell me, I have been longing for you to fuck me like a man, and you don't even have a man size cock. I can't believe I let myself fall in love with you before I knew if you would be able to fuck me into oblivion. I started to get up and find my clothes, obviously this was not going to work out. As I pulled my pants up she stopped me and made me look into her face, didn't you hear what I said, I have fallen in love with you. I am upset your cock is so small and it will never satisfy me but that doesn't mean I don't love you. We kissed and we kissed deeply as her tongue probed my mouth and she wrapped her arms around me. She pulled me back down to the couch and once again my face was in her crotch and licking her to a third, fourth and fifth orgasm. You are the best pussy licker I have ever had, you are better at then even my girlfriends. When she was finally satisfied with her own pleasure, she switched places with me and with pants off again she examined my still hard cock very carefully. She tried to wrap her hand around it but it didn't work very well, she looked up at me and told me how cute the little guy looked. If we removed all your crotch hair it would make it look bigger, and it would be like I was playing with a little boy. She continued to make comments and I have to admit they were very exciting to listen to. She started jerking my cock off with just two of her fingers. I almost feel like I am playing with a big clit more then playing with a cock. Your balls are small too, your sack is almost like a seed pod instead of a mans balls. I felt her other hand squeezing my ball sack. I watched as she put her beautiful red lips to the head of my cock and simply sucked the whole thing into her mouth. It was the most amazing feeling having her wet warm mouth on my cock. It was much better then when I slid my cock into her pussy as this hole had tongue and she used it vigorously on the underside of the head of my cock. The suction of her mouth was pulling hard on my cock and it only took a few more moments before I was shooting my load into her mouth, she swallowed all of it. Looking up at me she told me she was surprised that I produced as much cum as I did, she figured she wouldn't even be able to tell when I came since my balls were so small.

We spooned that night and when we woke up we

took a shower together, I enjoyed being able to wash her body feeling her breasts which were exquisite, when she turned around she noticed my cock was hard again and said oh look pinky is up and wants to play. She soaped her hands up and jerked me off right there in the shower. I watched as she used a razor to shave her crotch and then her armpits, she then turned to me and was on her knees, she looked up and said its time to trim little pinky and she began to shave my crotch, it was very erotic watching a woman shave around your cock and balls, you have to have trust to allow that to happen. When she was done pinky as she called my cock so adoringly now was smooth and soft. When she stood up she told me to raise my arms and then proceeded to shave my armpits until they were as smooth as pinky. It felt weird to have no hair on my armpits. When she was done she rinsed off the razor and told me we can work on the body hair a little at a time.

We dried off and found ourselves back on the bed, her legs were up and she was pointing at her pussy, and I was on it, kissing and licking until she screamed out loud. You are just so good at that I can't believe how you make me cum with your mouth, it makes up quite a bit for your little cock, oh I mean pinky.

We were together for three months, and she told me she had a surprise for me as I walked into her house and took off my coat. She presented me with a box as I opened it I pulled out a silky pair of pink boy shorts, I told her they would look great on her, and she laughted and said no silly they are for you, well for you and pinky, now lets go to the bedroom and you can put them on and lick my pussy like you do so well. I was naked and in those pink panties in no time, between her legs and her pleasure began, when she was done she told me to lay back and she produced a back massager and proceeded to place it on my cock, the vibrations were exquisite and I shot my load in the pink panties, she laughed and giggled as cum came through the material. I am so glad I bought you ten pairs of them, now here is a new pair go and change.

She had me in panties full time after that, and before that week was out, my legs, chest and back were shaved clean, my body was now as smooth and soft as hers. It was like she was playing dress up with me, she treated me more and more like a toy or even a girlfriend instead of her lover, which I guess I really wasn't as we hadn't had actual intercourse since that first time. When I inquired about that she just simply said that it would be a waste of time to try that again she couldn't even feel pinky when I had put it inside of her.   I would accompany her on outings and before long I was waiting for her in the salon when she convinced me to have a pedicure and manicure done like she was getting, and made sure they painted my toe nails a pretty pink.

Now that your legs are shaved I am sure you will look as good as I do in stockings, and sure enough I had to admit that my legs in stockings looked hot, and they felt good upon my skin. I had thought everything was going too good and I was right one day I stopped by her house earlier then I had told her I would and when I let myself in I found her with her legs in the air with some guy fucking her. When I walked in and she saw me she told me to go sit in the chair in the corner until they were done. I sat down dumbfounded and watched as this guy fucked her good, he fucked her for thirty minutes and his cock was very large I was mesmerized watching it go in and out of her pussy. She screamed, she called out to god, she said things that I had never heard her say before. She never really looked at me too much as she was in her own world with this guy pounding her vagina like there was no tomorrow and she loved every minute of it.

When they were done, they kissed and he said something about having to go or he would be late back to the office. When he was gone she turned her attention to me, and asked me how my day was going. I couldn't respond, I didn't know what to say I just watched the love of my life get fucked. I hope your not to freaked out by what you saw, you know I love you, but your cock is just so small, every now and then I am going to need to have a real cock in my pussy so I can remember what it feels like to be fucked good. I didn't know how to tell you without hurting your feelings, this doesn't change anything between us, I love you, I don't love the men that I fuck because your cock is so small. It made sense, but at the same time my brain was screaming that it didn't. Are you wearing your stockings today like a good little sissy. That was the first time she had called me that and I didn't even catch it. Why don't you get out of those pants and do what you do best, without thinking I slid out of the pants and was standing there in my pink panties and stockings climbing onto the bed as I got between her legs it was then that I realized that a large cock had just left this place, her pussy was shining wet and it was covered in another mans cum, come on she told me you need to clean me up and make me cum three times and then I will suck pinky off for you. I could smell his cum on her pussy, and as I got just above her lips she pulled my head onto and my whole face got a big wet kiss of her juices and the cum that was on the outside of her lips. I heard her giggle and tell me to get to work. I closed my eyes and started to lick around the edges until she told me to put my tongue inside of her it was then that I got a mouth load of his cum, and it was tough but I swallowed it down, it made me feel like a dirty little whore. Of course pinkies reaction to it was this is turning me on. After her third orgasm, she checked to make sure I didn't miss any cum spots on her crotch, she greedily pulled my panties down and looked at my baby smooth crotch and my little cock standing straight up, I watched as she brought her lips down and proceeded to rape my cock with her mouth sucking and pulling on it and it only took a minute of that before I shot my load in her mouth, though this time she didn't swallow it like she had done in the past, she moved up my silky smooth body and began to kiss me and with her tongue in my mouth I got to taste my own cum as it rolled from her tongue onto my own and then down my throat. She smiled at me telling me she was proud at how quickly I took to cum eating, she had thought that I would have put up more of a fight walking in on another man fucking her. She told me how hot it made her knowing that I was in the corner watching her get fucked by a real man, knowing that I was sitting in the chair wearing panties and stockings under my clothing. After that she no longer tried to hide her fuck sessions, in fact one night we were watching television and she simply called this guy up and he came over and fucked her right on the couch next to me with the tv still on. She had even made me take his hard cock and put it in her pussy. Of course when he was done it was my turn to clean her up. It moved forward from that to where she would have me lay on the bed and the guy would fuck her doggie style with my face right below her pussy and the guys balls swinging over my face, this way when the guy came she could simply sit down on my face and the cum would be still hot and fresh as it dripped out of her pussy into my mouth. By that time I was now wearing corsets, and nighties and even high heeled shoes.

One evening there was a knock at the door and when I let one of her boys in to fuck her, she told him that she wasn't feeling well and really wasn't up for it. When the guy was getting ready to leave, she said if you really want to fuck you can fuck him, I was sitting on the couch wearing a short mini skirt, obviously a guy, and the guy was like ok. I was bent over the edge of the couch and she watched as this guy pulled my panties down, she tossed him a tube of lubricant and he proceeded to lube his cock up. She turned off the tv, this is going to be exciting, this will be your first real cock in your ass honey, look pinky is standing straight up. I felt a little pressure and then a lot of pressure and pain as this guy took my anal cherry, the pain was unbelievable and then the constant feeling of something very large being pushed very deeply into my ass this guy wasn't being very considerate of it being my first time he was really pounding me, and just as he shot his load in my ass little pinky shot his load in my panties. When he left I went to the bedroom and cried, I knew I wasn't gay but at the same time I had orgasmed by being fucked by a guy in the ass, it was so wrong and the humiliation was horrible. Later she came in and comforted me, and told me that it would get easier with time, and that the reason I was being so emotional was probably because of all the female hormones she had been giving me, hadn't you noticed that the bra's you have been wearing are getting snug, go look in the mirror. Sure enough when I removed the bra I realized I now had a set of tits on my chest, not big but definitely there.

We snuggled that night and she promised me that I would like being a girl full time, and that next week she would go back to my apartment and get some of my favorite things and that I could live with her full time now but I would have to do so as a girl. In fact she even had a job opening at her company that would be perfect for me, I would be a secretary. I went to sleep and dreamed about having my ass pinched in the elevator, and being on my knees blowing my boss after his lunch, or maybe being fucked in the ass in the copy room by the delivery guy. Yes life would surely be different after this.

My wife made me a slut

"You know honey I am starting to like this new side of you, here you are sucking on my toes while I play with myself, you cleaned the whole house, did the laundry, made me breakfast in bed, you even ironed all of my business suits. Did you fix the buttons on my jacket like I told you to?" She asked.

"Yes Madam, I stuck my finger with the needle a couple of times but I was able to get the new buttons attached as you instructed." I replied to my now domineering wife.

I continued sucking on each toe individually; I knew my wife liked it when I did that. I raised my eyes slightly so I could watch her rub her clit and slide a finger inside of her very wet opening between her legs. Her head was leaning back as she pushed herself over the edge into that place where there was only pleasure to be found.

Before she got dressed for work she inspected me to make sure that I was cleanly shaven from head to foot, made sure that my back and buttocks was smooth as a baby. I was not allowed to be away from her without having my chastity device locked in place. She always looked at me when she closed and clicked the lock and said. "This is for your own good you know that right?" I simply nodded my head, she didn't like me to speak too much she found my masculine voice to rough for her ears, and I had not mastered speaking in a young woman's voice as of yet, so she smiled when I nodded my head.

I also got dressed while she was putting on her make up. Fish net stockings was my usual for around the house, a small mini skirt that was just below my ass cheeks, a simple bra and with falsies in place so it appeared that I had an ample young woman's breasts and a blouse. When I finished buttoning my blouse I turned to see my wife holding what appeared to be a latex girl full head mask with all the appropriate slutty makeup already on it. I simply knelt on the floor in front of her as she worked the piece over my head and made sure it was properly in place, it was very snug against my skin so it looked almost natural, she then placed a wig on top of that which was also very snug and when I looked in the mirror I looked like the appropriate slut that my wife liked me to be.

"Ok now face down on the bed with you." She pointed at the four post bed and proceeded to lock me in place spread eagle. One thing she was very adamant about is not allowing me any free time while she was away I was always locked up somehow, in the past I had been placed in a dog cage, or chained to the pole in the basement. One time she chained me in the kitchen so that I could clean the kitchen from top to bottom I had to take everything out of the refrigerator and scrub it clean with nothing more then a toothbrush. It was unusual that she lock me up on the bed like this.

She never liked to think that when I was locked up that I was being idle and spread eagle on the bed so she placed the ten inch suction cup silicone cock to the bed in front of my face. "You keep practicing on getting the whole length of this down your throat, one of the most important things you can learn is to deep throat a cock." She smiled at me and kissed my cheek and left for work. After watching me scoot forward and begin licking and kissing the head of the long cock she slipped head phones over my ears and pressed play on the compact disc player, and then she left for work. There was a minute of silence and then I heard a very sultry woman's voice speaking into my ears, and into my brain as the conditioning began.

"You are such a pretty girl, you like having breasts, and you like sucking cock. You will do whatever your wife tells you to do. She is the boss, she controls you, you live to serve her. All you can think about is making her happy, and you will do anything to make her happy. You are such a sissy, dressed up as a girl, your cock is so inadequate to please your wife, and that is why it is locked up the way it is. You do not like your own, cock, the only cock you like are the ones your wife makes you suck, you want to suck more cock, you want your boy pussy to be penetrated by long thick cocks. The only way your little cock can cum is to have something big and hard in your ass. You want your wife to humiliate you by being fucked by real men, you are not a real man, you are a sissy man with a small cock."

This line of dialogue went on and on, over and over again. I continued inching myself forward sucking and lick the ten inch cock that was in front of me. I wanted to make my wife proud of me by showing I could suck the whole thing. It was strange how much different I thought about the whole thing now, all I wanted to do was make her happy. I know she enjoyed keeping me this way. The head of the fake cock was now fully in my mouth. The dialogue never ceased it was constant.

"You want your wife to be pleasured by real men, you will do as she tells you to without question. When your wife has been pleasured by a real man you will only have one desire and that is to clean your wife's cum filled pussy with your tongue. You want your wife to whip you, you want your wife to slap you, you want your wife to cane your ass until you can't sit down. You live for the feeling of giving yourself to your wife for her pleasure of bringing you pain. You want to keep your body clean shaven for her, just like a girl, you want to be your wife's girlfriend, you want her to let her friends treat you the same way. You want to feel a man shoot his hot load of cum in your mouth, you want to feel a man behind you pulling your sissy ass on to his cock."

Another inch of the fake cock was in your mouth and you could feel it touching the back of your throat. Trying to relax so your gag reflex doesn't kick in, you move ever so slowly pushing it further down your throat, but it is no use you start to gag and quickly slide back down releasing the cock from your mouth.

"You want to be displayed as a little slut for all to see and to use and to enjoy. You want to have breasts like a real woman, you want your wife to ask you if you want to have breast enlargement procedure, you want more female hormones so that your little sissy cock will stop working entirely, you want to have your balls slapped until they are swollen, you want your little cock be whipped, you want to have your nipples pierced, you want be a slut, you want to be a slut, you want to be a slut, you are a slut, you are a slut you are a sissy little slut."

That part went on and on as you started on the cock in front of you again, slowly licking it and kissing it and taking more and more of it in your mouth.

I never heard the front door open or my wife enter the house with her friends.

I felt hands lifting my skirt, when I tried to listen in between the dialogue I could hear my wife's voice. "You see I told you he was .... yes he will do anything............let me get him ready.................he sure will.

The next feeling was of delicate fingers in a latex glove, applying something to the crack of my ass, then I felt a single finger enter me. She had done this many times when she milked me, I was not allowed to touch my cock without her approval and she didn't give that very often so instead she would stimulate my prostrate and the built up cum in my balls would simply drip out. The second finger felt good, my little cock was now straining at the bars of the cage that it was in. The third finger entered and now she started rotating her hand stretching me the fourth and fifth fingers came at the same time, she didn't like it when I was to comfortable and she slid her whole hand into me causing me great discomfort and pain. She withdrew her hand and plunged it into my asshole again. The pain was immense as I felt tears well up and run down the inside of the mask. Then she was gone. The pain still reverberated through my whole body.

When she returned she scooted up and leaned against the back of the bed so she could look at me. She smiled down at her little slut of a husband; she took one of the pillows and slid it under my belly so my ass was now sticking up in the air.

The headphones were still playing in my ears so I couldn't hear very well what was going on in the room, but my eyes must have shown my worry, and my wife just laughed at me, knowing that I was scared about what was going on. Though my line of sight was rather limited I watched as my wife leaned over slightly away from the bed, her hand reached up and brought a very big cock into view as she began to lick and kiss the head of the semi rigid cock. All I could do was watch as she began to suck the cock of this person she brought home with her from lunch. As I continued to watch her suck on this man's large cock I felt the sting of something that struck my exposed ass. It all happened so fast that I didn't even have time to think about it when the second stinging sensation came through my body as again my ass was struck. I tried to pull myself together and prepare for what I was sure would be another one. Not being able to hear anything but the lady telling me what a sissy slut I was there was no way to prepare for the next strike since I never knew when it was coming, but it came over and over again until the tears were now running down the front of my slutty mask. My ass burned from the beating I was getting while all the time I watched my wife suck this man's cock until it was rock hard. Finally she stopped and so did the beating, my ass burned from the pain, my wife leaned back on the bed and simply smiled at me expressing true love for me in the only way she could. It was then I realized that what was going to happen next as the man and his big cock disappeared from my limited view. I felt him get on the bed and then I felt the head of his cock push my ass cheeks apart. He was not gentle with me at all and he slid his very large cock into my ass, it was bigger and longer then my wife's delicate hand. It took him about three or four thrusts before I felt his balls against my ass, the pain that radiated through my body was all encompassing. His strong hands were now above the waist line of my mini skirt and he was fully penetrating me with each thrust. He didn't simply leave his cock in my ass which would have been painful enough, he withdrew it fully and then fully thrust it back into me. Over and over again I felt him do this, and now he was riding my ass hard. I felt so humiliated as my wife watched smiling at me like she was giving me a present of sorts. It seemed like it went on forever as all I could do was endure the raping of my ass with his cock. Finally he thrust deeply into me and shot his load filling my ass with his hot cum. I practically collapsed on the bed as far as I could being restrained the way I was as he withdrew his cock from my asshole. I could feel his cum as it dribbled out of my ass and down onto my own scrotum.

I tried to relax as the adrenaline slowly fell away.

My wife still smiling at me lying next to me on the bed started hiking up her skirt. The second man with a cock of similar size which was already hard came into view, no cock sucking this time though, he was between my wife's legs and his cock was entering her very wet pussy. He began to kiss her passionately while he pumped his cock inside of her, she returned his kisses deeply, he reached down and ripper her blouse open sending buttons flying everywhere, with her tits exposed he began sucking on the nipples making then hard and erect. It was then that beating of my ass began again, this time I could tell it was the cane and not the paddle. I couldn't hear the whooshing sound but each time it landed on my skin, it was like being set on fire. All the while I could only watch as this second stranger fucked my wife, my wife was totally enjoying the experience she no longer looked at me at all but totally into the eyes of this man she had inside of her. When she heard the canning begin she smiled as she stuck her tongue into this other man's mouth. The second man was very strong with her and it didn't take long before he was breathing heavy and thrusting deeper into her and I watched as they both came together. The canning had moved from my ass which surely had welts up and down it to the backs of my legs, I knew I would look like a zebra before long. My wife held up her hand and the canning stopped, the man withdrew his cock from my wife shaking off the last of the cum that was still on the tip of his cock onto her clit. He stepped back and I could no longer see him. My wife once again looked down at me and this time she repositioned herself so her cum filled pussy was in front of my face. I knew what had to be done and began licking her pussy first just on the outside then working my tongue into the folds and then into her opening, it was then as the first of this strangers cum began to drip into my mouth that I felt one of there hands in a latex glove working there fingers into my ass, since my ass was recently fucked by a big cock they were able to start with three fingers, there hand was obviously not as delicate as my wife's. Again my asshole screamed in pain as he tucked his thumb in and slid his hole very manly hand into my assy. My wife was getting to orgasm again as the bulk of the second man's cum was pushed into my mouth and down my throat as she came one more time. The man behind me worked his hand in and out of my ass and without even realizing it I came myself feeling the cum squirt out of my sissy cock. My wife heard me moan into her pussy and instructed the man to remove his hand from my asshole. This time I did collapse fully on the bed. My wife kissed me and lifted the headphone off my ear and said she was going back to work and that she hoped I enjoyed lunch. She giggled in my ear, and told me that we will have to have lunch at this place more often.

I felt her touch my ass as she left the room and then I slept since I was exhausted, and I didn't even hear the lady in my ears telling me what a slut I was, because I knew I truly was a slut, and that my wife made me that way, and I loved her for it.

My wife's friend takes control

My name is Anthony, and I was getting ready to marry the girl of my dreams, her name was Susan and she was my everything, I would do anything for her, we truly loved each other. We had been dating for a few years and finally had set a date. I worked for her father in the field of advertising and she had done some modeling and was in between jobs at the time. I was so excited knowing that she was getting ready just in the next room. We were still a few minutes away from walking down the isle and I had decided to go and check on her, I didn't want to ruin the day for her so I just opened the door a crack to see her one more time before we were wed. I was very astonished at what I witnessed, there on the chair was my soon to be wife with her dress pulled up and her panties were pulled to the side and her best friend Alice down between her legs licking and fingering her pussy. I closed the door and tried to grasp what I had just seen, just standing there next to the door I could hear my Susan moaning as she came, I pushed the door open a little again and could see them straightening her dress and tongue kissing, and I heard her friend tell my Susan not to worry that she would always be there for her. In the next moment we were at the alter and both of us said I do and we were wed for better or worse. I just didn't know at that time which way it would be for me.

Years passed by and we had a good life, or at least I thought so, I did start to notice my beautiful Susan started to lose interest in sex all together. I tried to initiate conversations about it but she never wanted to talk about it. One day as I came home a little early from work I saw Alice's car in the driveway and upon entering the house I heard them in the kitchen talking, I made my way to the doorway and could hear what they were saying. "I don't know Alice, I am just not that interested in having sex anymore, its boring." Susan said. "Honey I always told you that you should have stayed single, that you could do a lot better then Anthony, from what you have told me his dick is below average so how can he satisfy you." Alice replied. "Oh it is not that, he tries his best but there just isn't the spice that there once was" Susan said. "I am sure I could spice up your little love life why don't you invite me to stay for dinner and we can drunk and have a threesome, I am sure your dud of a husband would be up for that and then I can lick your little pretty pussy into ecstasy and he would never be the wiser for it." Alice replied. I stepped away from the door and made some noise to indicate that I was home. As I walked into the kitchen to greet my wife and to say hello to Alice, Susan said "Hello honey I just invited Alice to stay for dinner." I said that is great idea.

The night wore on and after the first bottle of wine we were all a little tipsy. I put some music on as we started the second bottle of wine, we weren't even through half of the bottle when the subject started to turn to sex. Alice began to tell of some of her crazy escapades with multiple partners at the same time, she emphasized that it was always better when it was two women and one man. It was then that she sat down on the other side of my wife and I watched as her hand gently played with her hair whiles her other hand moved to her tits. It didn't take long before she was unbuttoning my wife's blouse and I was gently rubbing my wife's inner thigh while I kissed her on the mouth. I watched as Alice's bright red lips took my wife's nipple and sucked on it bringing it erect and then she gently nibbled on her nipple. My wife was becoming very aroused as my fingers gently parted her pussy lips and I could feel how wet she was becoming. At that time we all retired to the bedroom, as I got undressed my cock was hard and Alice looked at it and giggled saying is that all you got Tony, I figured your cock was huge to win Susan over. Susan was embarrassed "oh stop that Alice" she said. Alice laid down on the bed and my wife continued to kiss her as she crawled between her legs and I inserted my cock into my wife's pussy from behind. I fucked my wife until she told me to stop, she wanted to switch positions but she hadn't cum from me fucking her. Alice reached into her bag and brought out a very large strap on and stepped into it. It was a good ten inches of rubber cock to my six inches of real flesh. She turned to me and said why don't you go stand over there and watch your wife get fucked, I was dumb founded and stood there as she mounted my wife with the strap on. It didn't take long before my wife was starting to moan. I could hear Alice talking to her, telling her to look at her pretty little pathetic man watching another woman giving his wife a good fucking. Her cock was sliding deep into my wife and my wife was holding her legs up and open to let her push as much as she could of that big rubber cock into her. Her moaning was getting louder as she continued to look at me standing there with my now semi erect cock. Alice continued go ahead and tell him to play with his little dick, tell him how small it looks and how its hardly a cock at all. Then my wife still looking at me said just those words. "I want you to play with your little dick honey, it is so pathetic looking" Susan told me. For some reason this was a really big turn on for me all of a sudden and before I could even touch my dick it was rock hard again. "She how much he likes being humiliated, why don't you call him some more names" Alice said. All the while she continued to fuck my wife slowly and deeply with her big strap on. "You are such a shitty fuck, I never cum from your little cock, you might as well be a sissy, I should dress you up as a girl your cock is so worthless" Susan told me. On that last part I shot my load all over her tits and it was a big load for my little cock. "See I knew he would like being humiliated by his wife" Alice said as she smiled at my wife who was really into the fucking that she was getting. "Now there is one more thing you need to do Susan to make it complete and then you will be allowed to cum, you are going to have to tell him to clean his mess up with tongue" Alice said to my wife. "You little shit look at the mess you made, I didn't tell you that you could let that little sissy dick shoot its load, now you get down here and clean my tits with your tongue and lick all your cum up" Susan told me. I immediately bent down and began to lick my own cum off of my wife tits then I heard Alice say. "Now you can cum Susan" It began deep down inside of my wife and as she watched me lick my cum up she came like a wild stallion I could see her squirting back all over Alice before she collapsed from her orgasm. I couldn't believe what I had done and what I had seen. Alice continued to whisper ideas into my wife's ear about me and my wife didn't miss a beat in introducing those ideas. Before we went to bed that night I had received a spanking with my own belt for misdeeds of cumming on her like that. My ass was beet red when she was done. "Since you are so willingly being such a little sissy I want you to put one of my teddy's on to sleep in" She even made me sleep on the floor. As I lay there I could here her snuggling and kissing and continued her playing with Alice, this time I think she went down on Alice until she came.

The next day was Saturday and Susan made me make her and Alice breakfast in bed, I was still wearing the teddy and they both had a good laugh at my expense. They continued to talk as if I wasn't even there. "I can't believe how amazing that was last night" Susan said. "I told you that you just needed to have me spice things up for you, I have a whole bunch of ideas for you" Alice responded. "I can't wait to hear some of them, its like I have a new lease on life, what crazy things are in that head of yours" Susan said. "Well for starters I think you are going to have to lock his little sissy dick up in a chastity belt, he shouldn't be allowed to cum anymore unless you want him to." Alice said. "Aren't those archaic from the middle ages" Susan asked. "Not at all they have a complete line of modern chastity belts that women have been using to restrain there naughty little sissy husbands for some time now." Alice stated. "How do they work" Susan asked. "Well they completed surround his cock so he can't touch it and it restrains his cock from being able to get hard or erect, and his balls are all snug and tight as well. He will be able to do his everyday things but he won't be able to play with himself." Alice responded. I tried to speak up and say something but with my rock hard cock making the teddy stand up kinda gave away how excited I was. "You see this is exactly what the chastity device would prevent" Alice stated. She then came over and lifted the teddy and placing my cock in her one hand she proceeded to smack it in quick succession as I cried out from the pain, and I watched as my cock shrank back down. "There is so much you can do to entertain yourself with him now that he knows his place, you can beat him and cause him pain, you can dress him up like a little slut and fuck him in the ass with that strap on. Hell we can bring in real men and he can learn how to suck cocks hard for you." Alice said.

Over the next few months my wife took Alice's advice and instituted a number of changes in our married life. Alice would come over every so often to check up on her and her progress. My wife now had me in full sissy garb and was practicing regular cbt on me. She even made me higher Alice as my personal assistant, so that I could be continually abused at work and at home. Alice loved coming in the office in the morning and making me pull my pants down so she could see what panties, bra and stockings I had on then she would pull my panties down and give my balls a good spanking, she told me after the first spanking that after awhile I would beg my wife to remove my balls to stop the constant pain. Every hour like clock work she would come into my office make me stand up and kick me in the balls

The Confession

John and Erica had been married for a little over six years, when Jim knew it was time to come clean with her about his secret perversions.

"So let me get this straight" Erica started. "You secretly wear my panties and stockings under your clothes to work. That you have a strong desire to be humiliated sexually and you want me to be the dominant person in our relationship. Is that correct?" She asked. John hung is head in shame and simply said yes Erica that is what gets me off. "I will need to think about this for a little bit" she simply got up and walked away. John knew this had gone poorly and realized that nothing would be the same again.

Erica was out in the back yard having a cigarette when there neighbor Dan came over to the fence and started chit chatting with her. John knew that Erica had found Dan attractive when they first moved in a few years ago, but she would have never done anything about it.

John watched as they both were smiling and then Dan jumped over the fence and they both entered the house. "Honey I was just telling Dan here about what we were just talking about and I figured the best way to give you what you want is to get what I want." John watched as Dan put his hands on Erica's tits, feeling them through her blouse, and Erica's hands made there way down to Dan's hardening cock in his shorts. It wasn't long before Erica was on her knees pulling Dan's shorts down and taking his hard cock in her mouth. "Is this what you want to see

John, another man's cock in your wife's mouth and soon to be in her pussy? Is your little cock getting hard watching me do this?" She reached over and felt for John's cock. "Hell I can hardly feel your hard cock it's so small" Dan took Erica's head and drove her deeper onto his cock. Erica fondled Dan's balls while she took Dan deep in her throat. As Dan gently moved her back to a standing position so he could bend her over our pool table and fuck her from behind. "I was telling Dan that he can come over and fuck me anytime he wants from now on, since you will not be fucking me any more. In fact I am going to get you a chastity device and lock you little dick up so you won't be allowed to touch yourself either. .You fucked up big time buddy, you want to be humiliated well I am going to take any form of pleasure away from you, you may never get to cum again, at least not by touching yourself." Dan was now behind her pulling her shorts down and sliding his large hard cock into her pussy. "Yeah come on Dan, give me that big cock, I have wanted your cock since I moved into this house, it is a shame I didn't realize what a wimp my husband was before else I could have been getting your big cock for years." Dan was holding her by her hips driving his hard cock into her faster and faster, Erica was moaning aloud as she continued to insult her husband. "Oh you wanted this so much, I am not going to disappoint you because once Dan's cums inside my pussy you are going to thank him for fucking your wife and then you are going to lick his cum from my crotch." Dan kept pumping away into Erica and soon he was groaning and his thrusts were getting stronger until finally he shot his load into John's moaning wife. John watched as Dan's slick wet cock slid from Erica's pussy. Erica simply pointed at her cum dripping pussy and John crawled over and began to lick Dan's cum from her pussy. "I hope you enjoyed that because I am going to make your life a living hell from now on just like you asked for" Erica turned and walked Dan back to his house. John who still had Dan's cum in his mouth simply smiled and swallowed the last of it down his throat thinking to himself, maybe this worked out better then I thought it would.

A Note From the Author

Well here it is the end of another project, I get mixed feelings when I come to the end of a project, I enjoy writing so much that I am sad to be at the end but at the same time I know that now others will get a chance to experience my wonderful lustful and sometimes sadistic thoughts via the story or the assignment. I just have so much fun writing about the experiences I have with my own submissive play things, they are such good little boi's all dressed so pretty and they do whatever I ask of them, well they know they will be punished if they don't.

So now it is your turn to once again do what I ask of you.

I would like to hear from you, I am going to give you my personal email address so you can contact me so that I can get your feedback on the stories and the assignments and anything else you would like to tell me about. I would love to hear about your own stories and experiences, I just love it when I get email from the people who read my work, so don't hesitate to contact me, who knows maybe I will give you a special assignment just for you.

Write to me soon.......

Love

Mistress Jessica

Mistressjessica01@gmail.com

www.ingramcontent.com/pod-product-compliance
Lightning Source LLC
Chambersburg PA
CBHW070200290526

45789CB00002B/848